CARO
FOR CHOIRS
2

FIFTY CAROLS FOR
CHRISTMAS AND ADVENT

Edited and arranged by

DAVID WILLCOCKS
AND
JOHN RUTTER

MUSIC DEPARTMENT

OXFORD UNIVERSITY PRESS

WALTON STREET   200 MADISON AVENUE
OXFORD, OX2 6DP   NEW YORK, N.Y. 10016

Oxford University Press, Walton Street, Oxford OX2 6DP
London New York Toronto
Delhi Bombay Calcutta Madras Karachi
Kuala Lumpur Singapore Hong Kong Tokyo
Nairobi Dar es Salaam Cape Town
Melbourne Auckland
and associated companies in
Beirut Berlin Ibadan Mexico City Nicosia

© Oxford University Press 1970

ISBN 0-19-353565-3

Details of orchestrations for carols in the collections *Carols for Choirs*
1, 2, and *3,* are given in the *Oxford Music for Christmas* catalogue. The
carols in this book, for which orchestral accompaniments are available on
hire, are indicated by † in the Index of Titles and First Lines overleaf.

The gramophone record *Carols for Choirs* (OUP 150) contains 14
titles selected from the three collections, performed by the Bach Choir
with the Philip Jones Brass Ensemble, conducted by David Willcocks.

Printed in Great Britain
at the University Press, Oxford
by David Stanford
Printer to the University

PREFACE

Carols for Choirs 2 has been compiled as a companion volume to *Carols for Choirs 1* to meet the needs of choirs and choral societies wishing to perform complete services or concerts of carols without the inconvenience of handling a number of separate leaflets and books. A further fifty carols have been selected, many of them from traditional sources and newly arranged by the present Editors or in settings by other distinguished musicians past and present. Among the original compositions included are carols by Benjamin Britten, Richard Rodney Bennett, William Mathias and William Walton.

The ten years which have elapsed since the appearance of *Carols for Choirs 1* have seen a steady growth in the number of carol concerts given by choral societies, often with orchestral accompaniment. With the needs of these occasions in mind, the Editors have included a number of secular carols and also a generous proportion of carols which may be orchestrally accompanied if desired. Most of these accompaniments call for no more than modest orchestral resources, and many of them may be performed by strings alone; parts are available on hire.

Advent Carol Services have also grown in popularity, notably in schools and colleges where it is not possible to celebrate Christmas during term-time, but no generally accepted form of service has hitherto existed. The Revd. David Edwards, sometime Dean of King's College, Cambridge, has drawn up for this book an Order of Service based on the annual Advent Carol Service held in King's College Chapel, and has written a Bidding Prayer; the Matin Responsory (with which the service opens) and a number of carols suitable for Advent have also been included. Provision has thus been made for the needs of a complete Advent Carol Service.

Care has been taken to ensure that most of the carols included in the book lie within the capacity of the average choir and that as many styles and periods as possible are represented.

Note

O come, all ye faithful and *Hark! the herald angels sing* have been included in an appendix. Extended versions of these two hymns are contained in *Carols for Choirs 1*.

INDEX OF TITLES AND FIRST LINES

Where first lines differ from titles the former are shown in italics.

Carols suitable for unaccompanied singing are marked thus*.
Carols with orchestral material available on hire are marked thus†.

1. A BABE IS BORN I WYS

F. BAINTON

1. A babe is born I wys, This world to joy and bliss, His joy shall nev-er fade and miss, And Je-sus is his is his name, And Je-sus is his his name.

2. On Christmas Day at morn,
This little child was born
To save us all that were forlorn,
And Jesus is his name.

3. On Good Friday so soon
To death he was all done,
Betwixt the time of morn and noon,
And Jesus is his name.

4. On Easter Day so swythe
He rose from death to life
To make us all both glad and blythe,
And Jesus is his name.

5. And on Ascension Day
To heav'n he took his way,
There to abide for aye and aye,
And Jesus is his name.

The words, taken from an old MS. in Westminster Abbey Library, have been slightly modernised.
Wys = know of a certainty.   *Swythe* = quickly, instantly.
Reprinted from the *University Carol Book* by permission of H. Freeman & Co.

2. A CHILD IS BORN IN BETHLEHEM

(Puer natus in Bethlehem)

Vv. 1 and 2 DAVID WILLCOCKS
(V. 1 translated from the Latin)
Vv. 3 and 4 from *The Cowley Carol Book*

SAMUEL SCHEIDT (1587–1654)
edited by DAVID WILLCOCKS

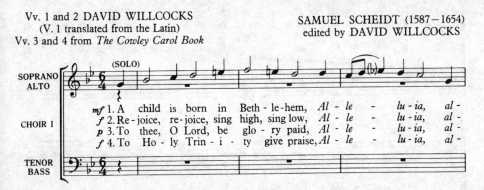

If preferred the piece may be sung a tone higher.
Also available separately (X144)
Verses 3 and 4 reprinted by permission of A. R. Mowbray & Co., Ltd.
Source: *Cantiones Sacrae Octo Vocum*, 1620

*orig. F (♮) not A

3. ADAM LAY YBOUNDEN

Words anon. 15th century

BOBORIS ORD

Allegretto (♩ = 108)

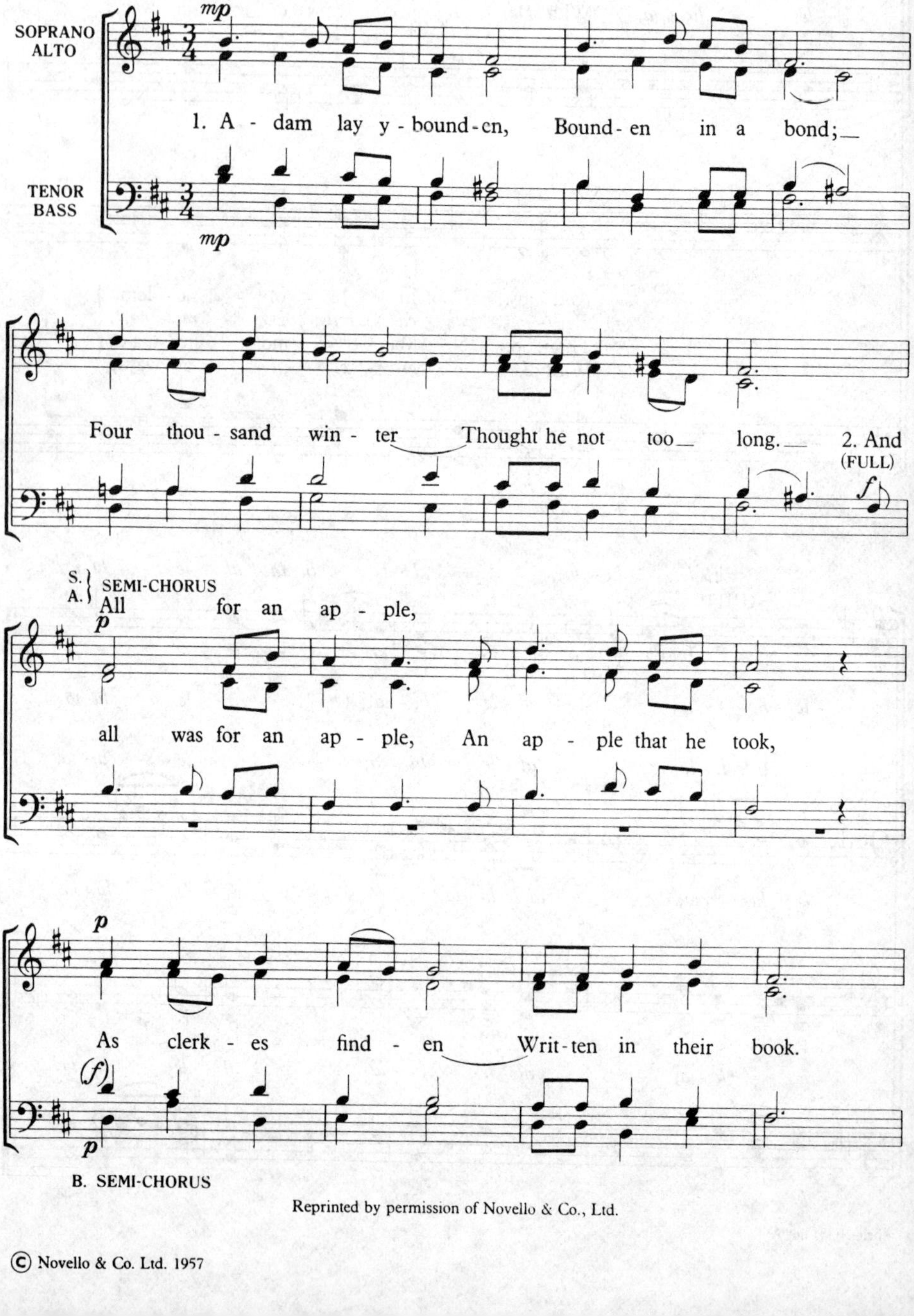

SOPRANO
ALTO
TENOR
BASS
mp
1. A - dam lay y - bound - en, Bound - en in a bond;—
Four thou - sand win - ter Thought he not too— long.— 2. And
(FULL)
f
S. A. } SEMI-CHORUS
p
All for an ap - ple,
all was for an ap - ple, An ap - ple that he took,
p
As clerk - es find - en Writ - ten in their book.
(f)
p
B. SEMI-CHORUS

Reprinted by permission of Novello & Co., Ltd.

3. Ne had the ap-ple tak-en been, The ap-ple tak-en been, ___

Ne had nev-er our ___ la - dy A - been hea-ven-é ___ queen.

4. Bless - ed be the time ___ That ap - ple tak - en was,

gra - - - - - - ci -
There-fore we moun sing-en, De-o gra - - ci - as, De - o
gra - - - - - - ci -

- as, De - o gra - - - - - ci - as!
gra - - ci - as, ___ De - o gra - - ci - as!
- as, De - o gra - - - - - - ci - as!

4. ALL MY HEART THIS NIGHT REJOICES

Words by PAULUS GERHARDT (1606–76)
tr. CATHERINE WINKWORTH

JOHANN GEORG EBELING
(1637?–76)

5. ALL THIS TIME

Words 16th century

WILLIAM WALTON

All this time this song is best: 'Ver - bum ca - ro fac - tum est.'

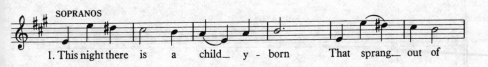

1. This night there is a child__ y - born That sprang__ out of

Jes - se's__ thorn; We must__ sing and say__ there - forn,

All this time this song is best: 'Ver - bum ca - ro fac - tum est.'

Words from *The Early English Carols* ed. R. L. Greene (Clarendon Press)

Also available separately (X201)

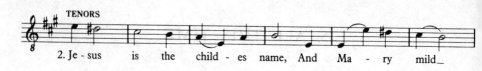

TENORS

2. Je - sus is the child - es name, And Ma - ry mild_

is__ his dame; All__ our sor-row shall turn__ to game:

All this time this song is best: 'Ver - bum ca - ro

fac-tum est.'___ 3. It fell__ up - on high mid - night: The star - res

SOPRANOS

shone both fair_ and bright; The an - gels sang_ with all__ their might,

All this time this song is best: 'Ver - bum ca - ro

6. NATIVITY CAROL

Words and music by
JOHN RUTTER

Also available separately (X169)

star____ He__ who loved__ us so.__   Far__ a - way__
rare,____ Hearts with his warmth he fills.__

si - lent he lay,_____ sempre cresc.

si - lent lay, _____ Born__ to - day,__ your hom - age

si - lent he lay,_____

si - lent lay,_____

(omit small notes on piano)

- day,   your   hom - age   pay;   Christ   is   born __ for

cresc.   *mp*

cresc.   *mp*

C   Back to p. 16.   D   (From p. 18)
for v. 3.   *pp espress. e dolce*

aye,   *pp*   Born __ on   Christ - mas Day.

4. Love   in   that   sta - ble   was

pp   C   Back to   *pp espress. e dolce*
p. 16. for v. 3.   D   (From p. 18)

pp   *mp*   *pp* (Salicional 8'
Celeste 8')

(Man.)   (Ped.)

born __   In - to   our hearts __   to   flow;   In - no - cent   dream - ing

7. DECK THE HALL

Words traditional

Welsh traditional carol
arranged by DAVID WILLCOCKS

1. Deck the hall with boughs of hol-ly, *Fa la la la la, fa la la la,*

'Tis the sea-son to be jol-ly, *Fa la la la la, fa*

'Tis___ the sea-son to be jol-ly, *Fa la la la la la la, fa la*

'Tis the sea-son___ to be jol-ly,

'Tis the sea-son *(Fa la la la la)* to be jol-ly,

la la la. Fill the mead cup, drain the bar-rel,

la la la la. Fill the mead cup, drain the bar-rel,

Fa la la la la. Fill___ the mead cup, drain___ the bar-rel,

Fa la la la. Fill___ the mead cup, drain___ the bar-rel,

Also available separately (X200)

★ Pronounce 'har' as 'ar' in *barrel*.

Cadenza ad lib.†, tempo rubato

★ Bracketed notes are optional.

† Conductors should feel free to omit the cadenza, or to substitute their own.

8. DING DONG! MERRILY ON HIGH

Words by
G. R. WOODWARD

16th cent. French tune
arranged by DAVID WILLCOCKS

1. Ding dong! mer-ri-ly on high in heav'n the bells are ring - ing: Ding dong! ve-ri-ly the sky is riv'n with an-gel sing - ing.
2. E'en so here be-low, be - low, let stee-ple bells be swung - en, And i - o, i - o, i - o, by priest and peo-ple sung - en.

Melody and words reprinted from *The Cambridge Carol Book* by permission
Also available separately (X196)

for E. T. C.

9. DOWN IN YON FOREST

English traditional carol
arranged by JOHN RUTTER

Melody and words reprinted by permission of Stainer & Bell, Ltd.
Arrangement from *Eight Christmas Carols* (Set 2)

I heard them ring: It's co-ver'd all ov-er with scar-let so red: And I

ring:_____   so red:_____

mf dim. pp   mf

Ah_____   Ah_____

Ah_____   Ah_____

Ah_____

love my Lord Je-sus a - bove a - ny - thing._____

dim.

Ah_____

3. At the bed-side there lies a stone:

The bells of pa-ra-dise I heard them ring: Which the sweet Vir-gin Ma-ry knelt up-on: And I love my Lord Je-sus a-bove a-ny-thing.

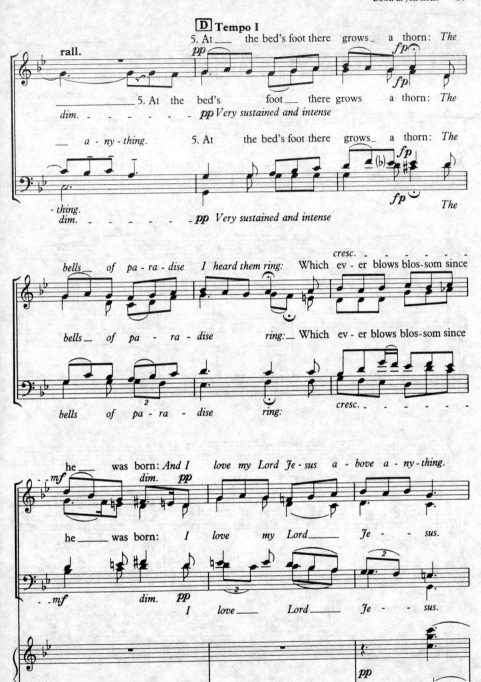

10. SHEPHERD'S PIPE CAROL

Words and music by
JOHN RUTTER

Available separately (X167)

Also available in the following arrangements:
1) S.S.A.A. voices (W76)
2) Unison voices with optional descant (U133)
3) Unison voices with easy accompaniment, shortened and simplified (U141)
4) Solo voice with slightly simplified accompaniment (Oxford Solo Songs)

shep-herd boy pi - ping On the way to Beth - le - hem.
hills__ so lone - ly On the way to Beth - le - hem?'

A legato
An - gels in____ the sky
An - gels__

brought this mes - sage nigh: 'Dance and sing for joy that
brought this mes - sage: 'Dance and sing__ for joy__ that

'I will find him soon   by the   star   shi-ning bright-ly

In the sky o'er Beth-le-hem.'_   An-gels in _ the sky

An - gels _

brought this mes-sage nigh: Dance   and   sing   for

brought this mes-sage: Dance   and   sing _   for

5. 'May I come with you, shep-herd boy pi - ping mer - ri - ly,

Come with you to Beth - le - hem?

Pay my hom-age too at the new King's cra - dle,

born this night in low - ly___ sta - ble yon - der,

Born for you at Beth - - - le - hem.'___

11. HAIL! BLESSED VIRGIN MARY

Words by
G. R. WOODWARD

Italian carol
arranged by CHARLES WOOD

1. Hail! Bless- ed Vir - gin Ma - ry! For so when he did meet thee, Spake migh-ty Ga-bri - el, And thus we greet _ thee. Come weal, come woe, Our hymn shall nev - er va - ry. Hail! Bless-ed Vir-gin Ma - ry!

2. A - ve, a - ve Ma - ri - a! To glad-den priest and peo - ple, The an - ge - lus shall ring from ev - 'ry stee - ple, To sound his Vir - gin-birth, Al - le - lu - i - a! A - ve, a - ve_ Ma-ri - a!

3. Arch - an - gels chant O - san - na, And Ho - ly, Ho - ly, Ho - ly, Be - fore the In-fant born of thee, thou low - ly, Aye - mai - den child of Jo - a - chim and An - na; Arch - an - gels chant O - san - na.

12. HERE WE COME A-WASSAILING

English traditional carol
arranged by JOHN RUTTER

From *Twelve Christmas Carols* (Set 1)

ALL VOICES
sempre **p**

- ley: Love and joy come to you, And to you your was - sail

too, And God bless you, and send you a hap - py New

Year, And God send you a hap - py New Year.

SOPRANOS
and ALTOS *mf gaily*

3. We are not dai - ly beg - gars that

mf

beg from door to door,_____ But we are neigh - bours'

child - ren Whom you have seen be - fore: *Love and joy come to*

you, *And to* *you your was - sail too,* *And God*

bless you, and send___ you a hap - py New Year, *And God*

send you a hap - py New Year._____ 4. Call up the but - ler of this house, Put on his gold - en ring;___ Let him bring us up a glass of beer, And bet - ter we shall sing *Love and joy come to you,___ And to*

you your was-sail too,___ And God bless___ you, and send___ you a

hap - py New Year,___ And God send___ you a hap - py New

Year.

mf espress.

5. We have got a lit - tle purse Of stretch-ing lea - ther skin; ___ We

want a lit - tle of your mon - ey To line it well with -

- in: Love and joy come to you, ___ And to you your was - sail

too, ___ And God bless you, and send ___ you a hap - py New

Year, And God send you a hap - py New Year.

F

SOPRANOS *f*

ALTOS *Ah* ___ *Ah* ___

TENORS and BASSES *f*

Ah ___ *Ah* ___

6. Bring us out a ta - ble, And spread it with a cloth;

f

8ve - - - - - - - - - - -

8ve _ _ ⌐

8ve _ _ ⌐

you,___ And God send_____ you   a

you,   And God send_____ you   a

too,   And God bless you, and   send__ you   a   hap - py New

8ve -

dim. - - - - *mf*

hap - py New Year,_ And God send_ you a   hap - py New   Year.__7. God

dim. - - - - *mf*

hap - py New Year, And God send you   a   hap - py New   Year. 7. God

dim. - - - - *mf*

Year,   And God send   you a   hap - py New   Year._____ 7. God

p

(8ve) - - - - - - - - - - - - - - - - - - - :

TENORS and BASSES

8. Good mas - ter and good mis - tress, While you're sit - ting by the fire, _____ Pray think of us poor child - ren Who are wand - 'ring in the

BASSES ONLY

mire: *Love and joy come to you, And to you your was - sail*

too, And God bless you, and send_ you a hap - py New

Year, And God send you a hap - py New

Year.

13. A NEW YEAR CAROL

★Words anon.

BENJAMIN BRITTEN

1. Here we bring new wa - ter from the well____ so clear,
2. Sing __ reign of Fair __ Maid, with gold up - on her toe,
3. Sing __ reign of Fair __ Maid, with gold up - on her chin,

For to wor - ship God with, this hap - py New Year.
O - pen you the West Door, and turn the Old Year go. } Sing
O - pen you the East Door, and let the New Year in.

★From *Tom Tiddler's Ground* — Walter de la Mare
Reprinted by permission of Boosey and Hawkes Music Publishers Ltd., London

REFRAIN (for verses 1 & 2)

le - vy dew, sing le - vy dew, the wa - ter and the wine; The

se - ven bright gold wires and the bu - gles that do shine.

D.S. %

REFRAIN (for verse 3)

le - vy dew, sing le - vy dew, the wa - ter and the wine; The

una corda

se - ven bright gold wires and the bu - gles that do shine.

c

14. HOW FAR IS IT TO BETHLEHEM?

Words by
FRANCES CHESTERTON

English traditional melody
arranged by DAVID WILLCOCKS

Words reprinted by permission of A. P. Watt & Son
Also available separately (W92)

© Oxford University Press 1970

5. Great kings have pre-cious gifts, And we have naught, Lit-tle smiles and

5. Great kings have pre-cious gifts, And we have naught, Lit-tle smiles and

lit-tle tears Are all___ we brought. 6. For all wea-ry chil-dren

6. For all wea-ry chil-dren

tears___ Are all___ we brought. 6. For all wea-ry chil-dren

(6.) Ma-ry must weep. Here, on his bed of straw
(7.) Babes in the byre, Sleep, as they sleep who find

(6.) Ma-ry must weep.___ Here, on___ his bed of straw___
(7.) Babes in the byre,___ Sleep, as___ they sleep who find___

Fine

Sleep, chil-dren, sleep. 7. God in his mo-ther's arms,
Their heart's de-sire.

Sleep,___ chil-dren, sleep. 7. God in his mo-ther's arms,
Their ___ heart's___ de-sire.

15. MATIN RESPONSORY

Words translated from the
First Responsory of Advent Sunday
in the Office of Matins
(early medieval Roman rite)

Adapted from a Magnificat
by PALESTRINA
(as sung at the Advent Carol Services
in King's College Chapel, Cambridge)

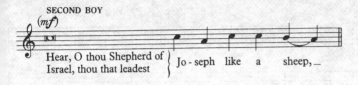

SECOND BOY
(mf)

Hear, O thou Shepherd of Israel, thou that leadest } Jo-seph like a sheep,—

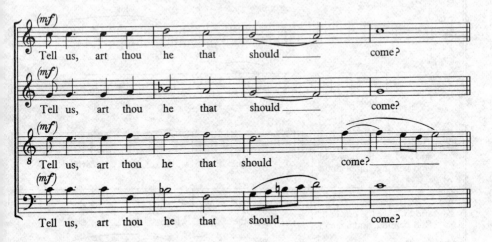

(mf) Tell us, art thou he that should _____ come?

(mf) Tell us, art thou he that should _____ come?

(mf) Tell us, art thou he that should come?_____

(mf) Tell us, art thou he that should_____ come?

FULL BOYS
(f)

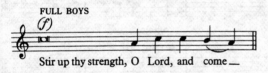

Stir up thy strength, O Lord, and come—

(f) to reign over thy peo - ple Is - ra - el.

(f) to reign over thy peo - ple— Is - - - ra - el._____

(f) to reign over thy peo - ple Is - ra - - - - - - el.

(f) to reign over thy peo - ple Is - ra - - el._____

CANTOR
(f)

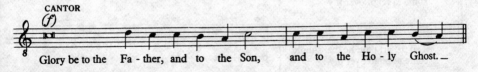

Glory be to the Fa - ther, and to the Son, and to the Ho - ly Ghost.—

16. COME, THOU REDEEMER OF THE EARTH

(Veni, Redemptor gentium)

ST AMBROSE (340–397)
tr. J. M. NEALE and others

Traditional melody
adapted by M. PRAETORIUS (1571–1621)
arranged by DAVID WILLCOCKS

Also available separately (*Six Christmas Hymns* arr. David Willcocks)

★ Verse 1 may be sung unaccompanied.

© Oxford University Press 1970

VERSES 2–7★

CHOIR
and
ORGAN

2. Be - got - ten of __ no hu - man __ will, But of __ the
3. The vir - gin womb that bur - den __ gained With vir - gin

Spi - rit, thou __ art __ still The _ Word _ of God ___ in _
ho - nour all __ un - stained; The _ ban - ners there ___ of _

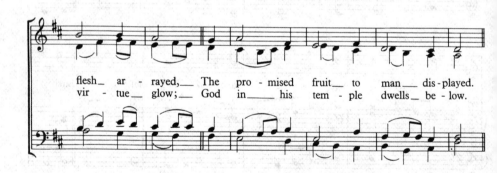

flesh _ ar - rayed, __ The pro - mised fruit __ to man __ dis - played.
vir - tue _ glow; __ God in ___ his tem - ple dwells _ be - low.

4. Forth from his chamber goeth he,
That royal home of purity,
A giant in twofold substance one,
Rejoicing now his course to run.

5. From God the Father he proceeds,
To God the Father back he speeds;
His course he runs to death and hell,
Returning on God's throne to dwell.

6. O equal to thy Father, thou!
Gird on thy fleshly mantle now;
The weakness of our mortal state
With deathless might invigorate.

7. Thy cradle here shall glitter bright,
And darkness breathe a newer light,
Where endless faith shall shine serene,
And twilight never intervene.

★ Verses 2 and 3 may be omitted.

VERSE 8

DESCANT (SOPRANOS)

8. All laud,— e - ter - nal Son,— to thee—Whose ad -

★ *8. All laud— to God— the Fa - ther be,— All praise,*

ALL OTHER VOICES

8. All laud, e - ter - nal Son, to thee Whose ad - vent

★ *8. All laud to God the Fa - ther be, All praise, e -*

ORGAN

Gt.+ Sw.

Tuba *f*

Ped.

- vent sets — thy peo-ple free, Whom with — the Fa - ther we —

— e - ter - nal Son, to thee: All glo - ry, as — is ev -

sets — thy peo - ple free, Whom with the Fa - ther we a -

- ter - nal Son, to thee: All glo - ry, as is ev - er

— a-dore, And Ho - ly Ghost for ev - er-more. A - men.

- er meet, To God the Ho - ly Pa - ra-clete. A - men.

- dore, And Ho - ly Ghost for ev - er - more. A - men.

meet, To God the Ho - ly Pa - ra - clete. A - men.

★ Alternative version of v. 8 (as given in *The English Hymnal*)

17. IL EST NÉ LE DIVIN ENFANT

(Born on earth the divine Christ Child)

English words by
JACQUELINE FROOM

French traditional carol
arranged by JOHN RUTTER

From *Eight Christmas Carols* (Set 1)

TENORS *mp*

-vè - ne - ment.   1. De - puis plus de qua - tre mille ans
Sa - viour mild.   *1. 'Tis four thou - sand years and more*

Nous le pro - met -taient les pro - phè - tes,   De - puis plus de qua-
Men his birth have been pro - phe - sy - ing;   'Tis four thou - sand

poco rit.

-tre mille ans   Nous at - ten - dions cet heur - eux temps.
years and more   While we longed for the joys in store.

B a tempo
p

Il est né le di - vin en - fant,   Jou - ez haut-bois, ré - son-
Born on earth the di - vine Christ Child,   O - boes, re - joice, with

fp   *fp*

fp (T.B. hum)   *fp*

B a tempo

p

Jou - ez haut - bois, ré - son - nez mu - set - tes; Il est né le di -
O - boes, re - joice, with_ bag - pipes vy - ing; Born on earth the di -

- ez haut - bois, ré - son - nez mu - set - tes;
o - boes, re - joice, with bag - - - pipes vy - ing;

- vin en - fant, Chan - tons tous son a - vè - ne - ment.
- vine Christ Child, Sing to_ wel - come the Sa - viour mild.

Chan - tons son a - vè - ne - ment.
Come wel - - - come the Sa - viour mild.

TENORS and BASSES   *mp legato*

3. Une é - ta - ble est son loge - ment,
3. *In a sta - ble ___ here on earth,*

Un peu de paille est ___ sa cou - chet - te; Une é - ta - ble est
Je - sus, ___ in the ___ man - ger ly - ing, In a sta - ble ___

son loge - ment, Pour un Dieu quel ___ a - baisse - ment!
here on earth, O how low - ly our Sa - viour's birth!

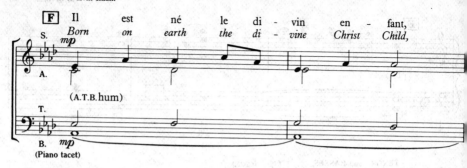

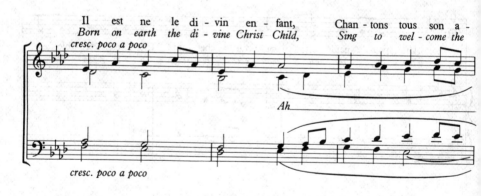

18. I SAW A MAIDEN

Words 15th century (adapted)

Old Basque Noël
with refrain added by
EDGAR PETTMAN

1. I saw a mai-den sit-ten and sing:
2. This ve-ry Lord he made al-le thing:
3. There was mick-le me-lo-dy at that child-es birth:
4. An-gels sang that night and said-en to that child:
5. Pray we to that child and to his mo-ther dear,

She lull-ed a child, a swee-te Lord - ing.
Of lord-es the Lord, of king-es the King.
And all in hea-ven's bliss, they ma-de mick-le mirth.
Now blest be thou and she, both meek and mild.
His bless-ing to them that mak-en now cheer.

Lul - lay, lul-lay, my dear son, my sweet-ing. Lul-lay, lul-lay, my dear heart, my own dear dar - ling.

Alternative version of text (as given in *The University Carol Book*)

1. I saw a maiden sitting and sing,
   She lull'd her child a little Lording.

   Lullay, lullay, my dear son, my sweeting.
   Lullay, lullay, my dear son, my own dear dearing.

2. This very Lord, He made all things,
   And this very God, the King of all Kings.

3. There was sweet music at this child's birth,
   And heaven filled with angels, making much mirth.

4. Heaven's angels sang to welcome the child
   Now born of a maid, all undefiled.

5. Pray we and sing on this festal day,
   That peace may dwell with us alway.

Reprinted from *The University Carol Book* by permission of H. Freeman & Co.

19. MYN LYKING

Words 15th century

R. R. TERRY

The words of this carol are taken from the Sloane MS.: spellings are unaltered.
Reprinted by permission of J. Curwen & Sons Ltd.

cresc.   **dim.**   **rall.**

Lul - lay my dere herte, myn own dere der - ling.

Lul - lay my dere herte, myn own dere der - ling.

Lul - - lay myn own dere der - ling.

cresc.   **dim.**   **rall.**

a tempo   *Fine*

mf

mf SOPRANOS

3. There was mic - kle me - lo - dy at that chyld - e's birth.
4. An - gels bright sang their song to that chyld; Blyss -

molto rall.

cresc.   *1st time only*   **V. 3: D.S.**
(- - - -)   **V. 4: D.S. al Fine**

All that were in heav'n - ly bliss, they made mic - kle mirth.
- id be thou, and so be she, so meek and so mild.

cresc.

To my mother

20. I SING OF A MAIDEN

Words traditional

PATRICK HADLEY

21. IT CAME UPON THE MIDNIGHT CLEAR

Words by
E. H. SEARS

Traditional English tune
adapted by ARTHUR SULLIVAN
Descant and organ part by
DAVID WILLCOCKS

In moderate time (♩ = 92)

SOPRANO
ALTO

TENOR
BASS

1. It __ came up - on the __ mid-night clear, That glo-rious song of old,
2. Still through the clo - ven __ skies they come, With peace-ful wings un-furled;
3. Yet __ with the woes of __ sin and strife The world has suf-fered long;

From an - gels bend- ing near the earth To __ touch their harps of gold:
And still their heav'n-ly mu - sic floats __ O'er all __ the wea - ry world;
Be - neath the an - gel - strain have rolled Two __ thou-sand years of wrong;

'Peace on the earth, good - will to men, From heav'n's all - gra - cious King!'
A - bove its sad and low - ly plains They bend on ho - v'ring wing;
And man, at war with man, hears not __ The love -song which they bring:

The world in so - lemn still - ness __ lay To __ hear __ the an - gels sing.
And ev - er o'er its __ Ba - bel __ sounds The __ bless-ed an - gels sing.
O hush the noise, ye __ men of __ strife, And __ hear __ the an - gels sing!

Also available separately (*Six Christmas Hymns* arr. David Willcocks)

(to next page for v. 4)

22. THE CHERRY TREE CAROL

English traditional carol
arranged by DAVID WILLCOCKS

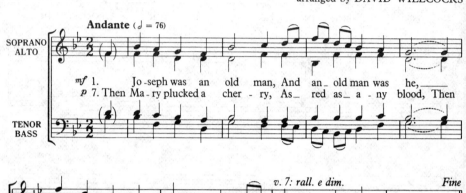

SOPRANO
ALTO

mf 1.   Jo-seph was an old man, And an_ old man was he,___
p 7. Then Ma-ry plucked a cher-ry, As_ red as_ a-ny blood, Then

TENOR
BASS

v. 7: rall. e dim.   *Fine*

When he mar-ried Ma - ry In the land of Ga-li - lee.
Ma-ry went she home - wards All_ with her hea - vy load.

2. And as they were walk - ing Through an_ or - chard so good,

mp

p

A. T. B. *Ah*_____ *Ah*___

p

Where were cher-ries and ber - ries As_ red as a-ny blood.

Also available separately (X197)

1st SOPRANOS

p 3. O then be-spoke Ma - ry, With words both meek and mild,
mf 5. Then bowed down the high-est tree Un - to— our La - dy's hand;

2nd SOPRANOS

V. 3: *pp* Ah_____ Ah___
V. 5: *mp*

ALTOS

V. 3: *pp* Ah_____ Ah___
V. 5: *mp*

'Pluck me— one cher-ry, Jo - seph; For— that I am with child.'___
'See,' Ma-ry cried, 'see,— Jo - seph, I have cher-ries at com - mand.'___

TENORS *mp*

Ah___

BARITONES *mf*

4.   'Go to the tree then, Ma - ry, And it— shall bow to thee; And
6. 'O   eat   your cher-ries, Ma - ry, O— eat— your cher-ries now;   O

BASSES *mp*

Ah_____ Ah___

after v. 6: D.C. for v. 7

Ah___

you shall ga - ther cher - ries By— one, by two, by three.'___
eat your cher - ries, Ma - ry, That grow up - on the bough.' ___

23. MASTERS IN THIS HALL

Words by
WILLIAM MORRIS

French traditional carol
arranged by DAVID WILLCOCKS

*The dynamic level of the refrain is in each case the same as that of the verse preceding it.
Also available separately (X208)

SOPRANOS and ALTOS

mp 2. Go - ing o'er the hills,___ Through the milk - white snow,___
mf 4. Quoth I, 'Fel - lows mine,___ Why this guise sit ye?___
mf 5. 'Shep- herds should of right___ Leap and dance and sing,___

mp

D.S. *for* REFRAIN

Heard I ew - es bleat___ While the wind did blow:
Mak - ing but dull cheer,___ Shep - herds though ye be?'
Thus to see ye sit,___ Is a right strange thing':

TENORS and BASSES

pp 3. Shep - herds ma - ny an one___ Sat a - mong the sheep,___ To
mf 6. Quoth these fel - lows then,___ 'To Beth - lem town we go,___ To

v. 3: pp
v. 6: mp

D.S. *for* REFRAIN

No man spake more word___ Than they had been a - sleep:
see a might - y lord___ Lie in man - ger low':

mf SOPRANOS and ALTOS

7. 'How name ye this lord,_____ Shep-herds?' then said I,_____

mf

mf TENORS and BASSES

D.S. for REFRAIN

'Ve - ry God,' they said,_____ 'Come from hea - ven high':

ff ALL VOICES

8. This is Christ the Lord,_____ Mas - ters, be ye glad!_____

f

(straight on for REFRAIN)

Christ-mas is come in,_____ And no folk should be sad:

(ALL VOICES)

Now - ell! Now - ell! Now - ell! Now - ell sing we clear! Holp - en

S. are all folk on earth,— Born— is God's Son so dear:— Now-

A. are all folk on earth,— Born— is God's Son so dear:—

T. are all folk on earth,— Born— is God's Son so dear:— Now-

B. are all folk on earth,— Born— is God's Son so dear:—

24. NOËL NOUVELET

(Nowell, sing nowell)

English words by JOHN RUTTER

French traditional carol
arranged by JOHN RUTTER

From *Twelve Christmas Carols* (Set 2)

Chan - tons No - ël pour le roi nou - ve - let.
Sing we no - well, a new King born to - day.

No - ël nou-ve - let, No - - ël chan-tons i - ci.
No-well, sing no - well good peo - ple ga-thered here.

TENORS *mf legato*

2. L'an - ge di - sait: 'Pas - teurs, par - tez d'i - ci
2. Un-to hum-ble shep - herds came the an - gel near;

sempre cantabile

L'â - me en re - pos et le coeur ré-jou - i; En Beth-lé -
'Hence', said he, 'to Beth - lem, be ye of good cheer. Seek there the

S. La crèche é - tait au lieu d'un ber - ce - let,
Heav'n's might-y Lord all cra-dled in the hay,

A. La crèche é - tait au lieu d'un ber - ce - let,
Heav'n's might-y Lord all cra - dled in the hay,

D

S.A. No - ël nou - ve - let, No - ël chan-tons i - ci.
No-well, sing no - well, good peo - ple__ ga-thered here.

mp   *p*

TENORS and BASSES *mf*

4. Bien - tôt les rois, par l'é - toile__ é - clair - cis
4. *East-ern sa - ges seek him, in the dark-ness drear*

mp   *p   p   p   p*

dim.   *p*

De__ l'o - rient dont ils é - taient sor - tis A Beth - lé -
By a star il - lu - mined shin-ing forth so clear, Guid - ing__

p   p   p   p   p

25. SANS DAY CAROL

Cornish traditional carol
arranged by JOHN RUTTER

Words collated by Percy Dearmer and used by permission of Oxford University Press
Arrangement from *Twelve Christmas Carols* (Set 2)

ALL VOICES

Ma - ry bore_ Je - sus, who died on the cross: And_

Jesus Christ

Ma - ry bore_ Je - sus our Sa - viour for to be,___ And the

cresc. _mf_

cresc. _mf_
(Piano tacet)

first_ tree in the green-wood, it was the hol - ly,___ hol - ly,___ hol -

- ly! And the first tree in the green-wood, it___ was_ the_ hol - ly!

mp

TENORS and BASSES *p ma sonore*

3. Now the hol-ly bears a ber-ry as black as the coal, And Ma-ry bore Je-sus, who died for us all:

S. A. *Ah*
T. *And*
B. *Ah*

Ma-ry bore Je-sus Christ our Sa-viour for to be,
Ah

And the

cresc.

(Piano tacet)

cresc.

S. hol-ly, hol-

first tree in the green-wood, it was the hol-ly,

Ah

A. *Ah*

Ah

Ah

26. SIR CHRISTÈMAS

Words anon. (*c.* 1500)

WILLIAM MATHIAS

No-well, no-well,   no-well, no-well,

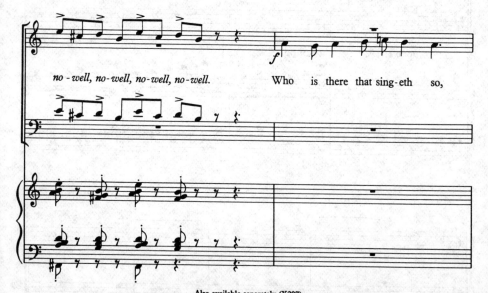

no - well, no-well, no-well, no-well.   Who   is   there   that   sing-eth   so,

Also available separately (X207)

This carol is from *Ave Rex*, a carol sequence by William Mathias (O.U.P.) commissioned
by the Cardiff Polyphonic Choir.

No-well, no-well,   no-well, no-well?

f I   am here, Sir Chris-tè-mas, Sir

Chris-tè-mas, Sir Chris-tè-mas.

Wel-come, my lord— Sir Chris-tè-mas!

Sw. *f*

Man.

Wel-come to all,— both more and less, Come near,   come near,   come

sing with us now joy - ful - ly,_____ joy - ful - ly,_____ joy - ful - ly:_____

No-well, no-well,   no-well, no-well,   no-well, no-well, no-well, no-well,   no -

- well!_____   No-well!   (shout)

Man.   Ped.

27. O COME, O COME, EMMANUEL

(Veni, veni, Emmanuel)

Words 18th century
tr. T. A. LACEY

Melody from 15th century
French Franciscan Processional★
adapted and arranged by
DAVID WILLCOCKS

1. O come, O come, Em - ma - nu - el! Re - deem thy cap - tive Is - ra - el, That in - to ex - ile drear is gone Far from the face of God's dear Son.
5. O come, O come, A - do - na - ï, Who in thy glo - rious ma - jes - ty From that high moun - tain clothed with awe Gav - est thy folk the el - der law.

Re - joice! Re - joice! Em - ma - nu - el Shall come to thee, O Is - ra - el.

Also available separately (*Six Christmas Hymns* arr. David Willcocks)

★Paris, Bib. Nat. Fonds Latin MS. 10581
Congregation should sing sections marked ⌐ ⌐ of verses 1, 2, 4 and 5.
ⓒ Oxford University Press 1970   Words from *The English Hymnal* by permission of Oxford University Press

VERSES 2 and 4
TENORS and BASSES

f 2. O come, thou Branch of Jes - se! draw The quar - ry from the li - on's claw; From
f 4. O come, thou Lord of Da - vid's Key! The roy - al door fling wide and free; Safe-

Full Sw. p

Ped.

REFRAIN

T.

the dread ca - verns of the grave, From ne - ther hell, thy peo - ple save. Re -
- guard for us the heav'n - ward road, And bar the way to death's a - bode.

B.

the dread ca - verns of the grave, From ne - ther hell, thy peo - ple save. Re -
- guard for us the heav'n - ward road, And bar the way to death's a - bode.

cresc.

(♩)

f

after v. 2: straight on for v. 3
after v. 4: D.C. for v. 5

- joice! Re-joice! Em - ma - nu - el Shall come to thee, O Is - ra - el.

- joice! Re-joice! Em - ma - nu - el Shall come to thee, O Is - ra - el.

after v. 2: straight on for v. 3
after v. 4: D.C. for v. 5

VERSE 3

mf SOPRANOS and ALTOS

3. O come, O come, thou Day - spring bright! Pour on our souls thy heal - ing light; Dis -

Ch. flutes   *p*

(Man.)

S.

cresc.   REFRAIN   *f*

- pel the long night's lin - g'ring gloom, And pierce the sha-dows of ___ the tomb. Re -

A.

cresc.   *f*

- pel the long night's lin - g'ring gloom, And pierce the sha-dows of ___ the tomb. Re -

mf

cresc.   *f*

Back to p. 121 for v. 4

Em - ma - nu - el Shall come to thee, O Is - ra - el.

- joice!   Re-joice! Em - ma - nu - el Shall come to thee, O Is - ra - el.

- joice!   Re - joice! Em - ma - nu - el Shall come to thee, O Is - ra - el.

Back to p. 121 for v. 4

28. THE SHEPHERDS' CRADLE SONG
(Wiegenlied)

Tr. A. FOXTON FERGUSON

KARL LEUNER
arranged by
CHARLES MACPHERSON

Andante moderato e teneramente

29. OF THE FATHER'S HEART BEGOTTEN

(Corde natus ex parentis)

PRUDENTIUS (*b.* 348)
tr. R. F. DAVIS

Melody from 'Piae Cantiones,
Theoderici Petri Nylandensis', 1582
arranged by
DAVID WILLCOCKS

1. Of the Fa - ther's
3. He as - sumed this
5. This is he, whom

heart be - got - ten, Ere the world from cha - os rose,
mor - tal bo - dy, Frail and fee - ble, doomed _ to die,
seer and sy - bil Sang in a - ges long _ gone by;

Words reprinted by permission of J. M. Dent & Sons, Ltd.
Also available separately (E100)

© Oxford University Press 1963

He is Al - pha: from that Foun - tain   All that is and hath been
That the race from dust cre - a - ted   Might not per - ish ut - ter-
This is he of old re - veal - ed   In the page of pro - phe-

flows;   He is O - me - ga, of all   things   Yet to
- ly,   Which the dread- ful Law had sen - - - - tenced   In the
- cy;   Lo! he comes, the pro-mised Sa - - - - viour;   Let the

after vv. 1 and 3: straight on for vv. 2 and 4
after v. 5: to p. 131 for v. 6

come the mys - tic Close,
depths of hell to lie,   *Ev - er - more and ev - er - more.*
world his prais - es cry!

VERSES 2, 4

SOPRANOS (and ALTOS)

2. By his word was all cre - a - ted; He com-mand-ed and 'twas
4. O how blest that won-drous birth - day, When the Maid the curse re-

done;   Earth and sky and bound-less o - cean,   U - ni-verse of
-trieved,   Brought to birth man-kind's sal - va - tion,   By the Ho - ly

three in one,   All that sees the moon's soft ra - - - - diance,
Ghost con-ceived;   And the Babe, the world's Re - deem - - - - er,

D.S. for vv. 3 and 5

All that breathes be - neath the sun,   *Ev - er - more and ev - er - more.*
In her lov - ing arms re - ceived,

-e'er ye be, ye faith - ful, Let your

ye faith - - - - ful,

-e'er ye be, ye faith - ful, Let your

faith - - - - ful,

faith - ful,

joy - ous an - thems ring, Ev - 'ry tongue his name con-

joy - ous an - thems ring,_____ Ev - 'ry tongue his

30. THE TWELVE DAYS OF CHRISTMAS

English traditional carol★
arranged by JOHN RUTTER

Adapted from the arrangement in *Eight Christmas Carols* (Set 2).
Audience may sing melody line during sections marked ⌐ ¬.

★ Melody for "Five gold rings" added by Frederic Austin, and reproduced by
permission of Novello & Co. Ltd.

© Oxford University Press 1970

4

fourth day of Christ-mas my true love sent to me   Four   call-ing birds,

three   French hens,   two   tur-tle doves and a   par - tridge in a pear

5

tree.   On the   fifth__ day of Christ-mas my true love sent to me____

Five gold ____ rings, _____ four _ call-ing birds, three French hens,

two _ tur-tle doves and a par-tridge in a pear tree. On the

sixth _ day of Christ-mas my true love sent to me

BASSES DIV.

Six geese a-lay-ing,

Sev'n swans a-swim-ming, six geese a-lay-ing, five gold____ rings,_____ four__ call-ing birds, three French hens, two __ tur-tle doves and a par-tridge in a pear tree. On the

eighth day of Christ-mas my true love sent to me   Eight maids a - milk-ing,

sev'n swans a-swim-ming, six geese a - lay-ing, five   gold__ rings,__

four__ call - ing birds,   three French hens,   two__ tur - tle doves and a

par - tridge in a pear tree.   On the ninth day of Christ-mas my

true·love sent to me   Nine la - dies danc-ing, eight maids a - milk-ing,

sev'n swans a-swim-ming, six geese a - lay -ing,   five   gold__

five gold _ rings, ___ four _ call-ing birds, three French hens,

two tur-tle doves and a par-tridge in a pear tree.   On the

molto allargando

12 **Maestoso**

twelfth day of Christ-mas my true love sent to me

Maestoso

Tempo I (fast)

Twelve drum - mers drum - ming, 'lev'n pi - pers pi - ping,

ten lords a - leap - ing, nine la - dies danc - ing,

eight maids a - milk - ing, sev'n swans a - swim - ming,

148

31. ONCE IN ROYAL DAVID'S CITY

Words by
C. F. ALEXANDER

H. J. GAUNTLETT
Vv. 1–5 harmonised by A. H. MANN
Descant and organ part by DAVID WILLCOCKS

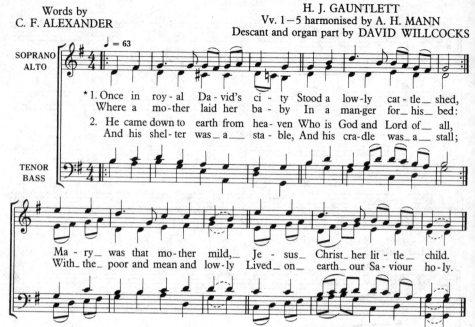

3. And through all his wondrous childhood
   He would honour and obey,
   Love and watch the lowly maiden,
   In whose gentle arms he lay:
   Christian children all must be
   Mild, obedient, good as he.

4. For he is our childhood's pattern,
   Day by day like us he grew,
   He was little, weak, and helpless,
   Tears and smiles like us he knew:
   And he feeleth for our sadness,
   And he shareth in our gladness.

5. And our eyes at last shall see him,
   Through his own redeeming love,
   For that child so dear and gentle
   Is our Lord in heaven above;
   And he leads his children on
   To the place where he is gone.

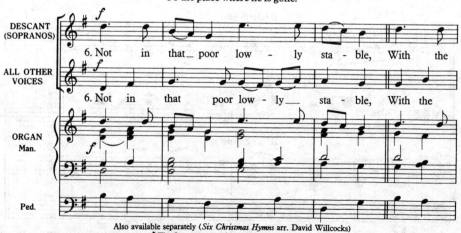

Also available separately (*Six Christmas Hymns* arr. David Willcocks)
* The first verse may be sung by a solo treble.
Harmonisation for vv. 1–5 reprinted by permission of Novello & Co. Ltd.
© Oxford University Press 1970 (descant and organ part)

ox - en stand - ing by, We shall see__ him; but in

ox - en stand - ing__ by, We shall see him; but__ in__

hea - ven, Set at God's__ right hand on high; Where__ like

hea - ven, Set at God's right hand__ on__ high; Where like

stars his chil - dren crowned All__ in white shall wait a - round.

stars his child - ren crowned All in white shall wait__ a - round.

cresc.

cresc.

cresc.

for Michael Nicholas and the Choir of St. Matthew's Church, Northampton

32. OUT OF YOUR SLEEP

Words: 15th century, anon.

RICHARD RODNEY BENNETT

1. Out of your sleep a - rise and wake, For

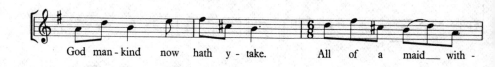

God man - kind now hath y - take. All of a maid___ with -

- out a - ny make; Of all___ wo - men she bear - eth the bell.___

2. And through a mai - dè fair _ and wise, Now man is made of

full___ great price; Now an - gels kne - len to man's

No. 2 of *Five Carols*, reprinted by permission of Universal Edition

ser - vice, And at this time_ all this_ be - fell._____ 3. Now

2 SOPRANO and TENOR

man is bright - er than the sun; Now

man in heav'n on high shall won; Bless - èd be God_ this

game is be - gun And his_ mo - ther the Em - press of hell.____

TUTTI **3**

_ 4. That ev - er was thrall_ now is_ he free; That ev - er was small now

great_ is she; Now shall God deem_ both thee and me Un - to his

bliss_ if we do_ well.____ 5. Now man he may to hea-ven wend; Now

heav'n and earth to him they bend. He that was foe_ now is our_ friend. This

is no nay_ that I you_ tell.____ 6. Now bless - èd Bro - ther

grant _ us grace, At doom-ès day to see_ thy face, And in thy

court_ to have a place, That we may there_sing thee no - well.

33. PAST THREE A CLOCK

Words by G. R. WOODWARD
(refrain traditional)

English traditional carol
arranged by JOHN RUTTER

Past three a clock, And a cold frosty morning: Past three a clock: Good morrow, masters all!

1. Born is a baby, Gentle as may be, Son of th' eternal Father supernal.

Past three a clock, And a cold frosty

Arrangement from *Twelve Christmas Carols* (Set 2)

Words, from *The Cambridge Carol Book*, are reprinted by permission of the S.P.C.K.

3. Mid earth re - joi - ces Hear-ing such voi-ces Ne'er-to-fore__ so__ well

voi - ces

Ca - rol - ling Now-ell. Past three a clock, And a cold__ fros - ty__

morn - ing: Past three a clock; Good mor-row, mas - ters all.

SOPRANOS
4. Hinds o'er the pear - ly de - wy lawn ear - ly Seek the high

1st ALTOS★
4. Hinds o'er the de - wy lawn ear - ly

2nd ALTOS
Hinds o'er the

8ve

legato

D
S. mf
stran - ger Laid in the man - ger.
A.
Seek the high stran - ger in the man - ger.
T.
Past three a clock, And a
B. mf
8ve
mf
mp
tr

cold fros - ty morn - ing: Past three a clock; Good mor-row, masters all!

tr   tr   tr   tr   tr

★or 2nd sopranos

6. Myrrh from full _ cof – fer In – cense they of – fer:

Nor _ is _ the _ gold – en nug - get with – hold – en.

Past three a clock, And a cold_ fros - ty_ morn - ing: Past three a

clock; Good mor-row, mas - ters all!   7. Thus they: I

7. Thus they: I   pray   you,

34. PERSONENT HODIE

Words from *Piae Cantiones*, 1582

German, 1360
arranged by GUSTAV HOLST

Reprinted by permission of J. Curwen & Sons, Ltd.

For English words, see *The Oxford Book of Carols*

'Bethlehem adeunt' has been substituted for 'Parvulum inquirunt' (which may well be a clerical error since no similar repetition of words is to be found in the other verses.)

© Gustav Holst 1924

35. QUELLE EST CETTE ODEUR AGRÉABLE?

(Whence is that goodly fragrance flowing?)

Tr. A. B. RAMSAY
(v. 4 tr. DAVID WILLCOCKS)

French traditional carol
arranged by DAVID WILLCOCKS

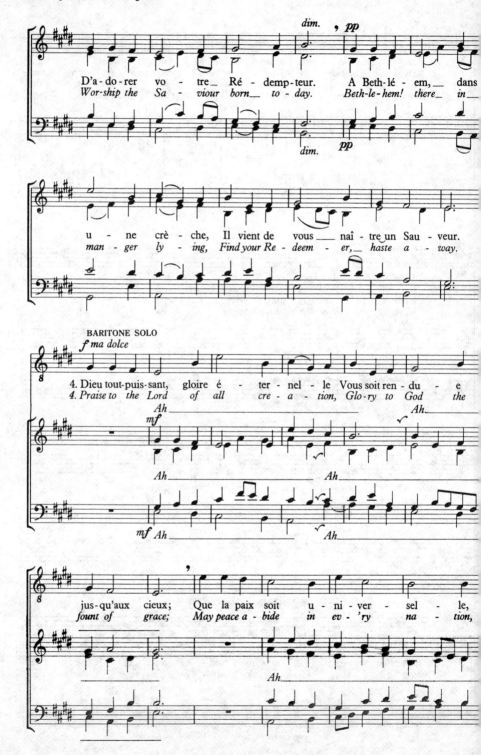

D'a - do - rer   vo - tre_ Ré - demp - teur.   A Beth-lé - em, _   dans
Wor-ship the   Sa - viour born_ to - day.   Beth-le-hem! there_   in

u — ne crè - che, Il vient de vous __ naî - tre un Sau - veur.
man - ger ly - ing, Find your Re - deem - er, _ haste a - way.

BARITONE SOLO

4. Dieu tout-puis-sant, gloire é - ter - nel - le Vous soit ren - du - e
4. Praise to the Lord of all   cre - a - tion, Glo-ry to God   the

jus - qu'aux cieux; Que la paix soit u - ni - ver - sel - le,
fount of   grace; May peace a - bide in ev - 'ry na - tion,

Que la grâce a - bonde en tous lieux. Dieu tout - puis -
Good - will in men of ev - 'ry race. Praise to the

- sant, gloire é - ter - nel - le Vous soit ren - du - e
Lord of all cre - a - tion, Glo - ry to God the

jus - qu'aux cieux.
fount of grace.

36. QUEM PASTORES LAUDAVERE

(Shepherds left their flocks a-straying)

Tr. IMOGEN HOLST

German, 14th century
arranged by JOHN RUTTER

English words reprinted by permission of G. & I. Holst Ltd.

Also available separately (X211)

Na - - tus est____ rex glo - - ri - ae.
'Christ____ is born____ in Beth - le - hem.'

S. A.   *p*

Ah _____   Ah ____

T. and B. *mp*

2. Ad quem ma - gi am - bu - la - bant, Au - rum, thus, myrr-
2. Wise men came from far,____ and saw him: Knelt____ in 'hom - age

Ah _____

- ham por - ta - bant, Im - mo - la - bant haec sin - ce - re
to a - dore him; Pre - cious gifts they laid be - fore him:

Ah _____

Na - - to re - - gi glo - - ri - ae.
Gold and frank - in - cense____ and myrrh.

Note: v. 2 may be sung by three solo voices.

Note: Choir I part in v. 3 may be sung by a solo voice, in which case Choir II should sing "Ah"

37. QUITTEZ, PASTEURS
(Come leave your sheep)

English words by JOHN RUTTER

French traditional carol
arranged by JOHN RUTTER

1. Quit - tez, pas - teurs, Vos bre - bis, vos hou -
1. Come leave your sheep, Your ewes with lambs a -

- let - tes, Vo - tre ha - meau Et le soin du trou -
- feed - ing, O shep - herds, hear Our mes - sage of good

- peau; Chan - gez vos pleurs En u - ne joie par -
cheer; No long - er weep; The an - gel ti - dings

From *Twelve Christmas Carols* (Set 1)

-fai - te; Al - lez tous a - dor - er _ Un Dieu, un
heed - ing, To Beth-lem haste a - way! Our Lord, our

Dieu, Un Dieu qui vient vous con - so - ler. Un
Lord, Our Lord is born this hap - py day. Our

Dieu, un Dieu, Un Dieu qui vient vous con - so -
Lord, our Lord, Our Lord is born this hap - py

- ler.   SEMI-CHORUS ★ *p*
day.   2. Vous
                                                                2. *He*

★A few sopranos and tenors, or solo voice

est,   il est,   Il est__ le fi - dèle ber - ger!__
*own,   now own   His faith-ful love re - vealed of   old.*__

dim.   C p

TENORS and BASSES
mp

3. Rois
3. Ye

pp

legato

d'O - - rient   L'é - toi - le vous é - clair - e; A
sa - ges   three   Ar - rayed in roy - al splen - dour, Your

p

ce grand   roi   Ren - dez hom-mage et   foi.   L'as - tre bril -
ho - mage   pay;   a king is born this   day.   The star ye

D

38. RESONEMUS LAUDIBUS

14th century carol★
arranged by DAVID WILLCOCKS

1. Re - so - ne - mus lau - di - bus__ cum jo - cun - di - ta - ti - bus__ ec - cle - si - am fi - de - li - bus. Ap - pa - - - ru - it__ quem ge - - - nu - it__ Ma -

★ transcribed and edited by Frank Ll. Harrison (from *Now make we Merthe*, Bk. 1—O.U.P.)
Also available separately (X210)

-ri - a.   5. Et De - o qui

-it Ma - ri - a.   5. Et De - o qui

(ALL VOICES)
ve - ni - as __ do - nat et lae - ti - ti - as __ nos e - i - dem

gra - ti - as. Ap - pa - - - ru - it __ quem

8ve brillante

ge - - nu - it __ Ma - ri - a. __

Full Ped.

39. THE ANGELS AND THE SHEPHERDS

Words adapted from
HELEN A. DICKINSON

Bohemian traditional carol
arranged by C. H. TREVOR

The angels

Moderato e leggiero (♩ = c. 80)

SOPRANOS

1. Shep - herds, O__ hark ye,__ glad__ ti - dings__ we__ bring,

poco rit.

Peace and__ good - will to__ the__ world now__ we__ sing;

Meno mosso

See in a man - ger Christ the An - oint - ed, Whom for your Sa - viour

Slow

God hath ap - point - ed. Al - le - lu - ia.

The shepherds

Poco meno mosso, leggiero

TENORS and
BASSES

2. In yon - der__ man - ger__ be - hold now__ he__ lies,

poco rit.

Whom an - gel - voi - ces__ fore - told from__ the__ skies.

Meno mosso

Seek - ing thy mer - cy, we kneel be - fore thee, Sing - ing thy prais - es,

Words used by permission of H. W. Gray Inc.

Also available separately (X 78)

humb - bly a - dore thee. Al - le - lu - ia.

The angels and the shepherds

3. Still through the a - ges the song doth re - sound,

3. Still through a - ges doth re - sound,

Peace and good - will on the earth shall a - bound;

Peace, good - will on earth a - bound;

Bear we the ti - dings to ev - 'ry na - tion, Born is the Christ Child

Al - le - lu - ia. Al - le -

for man's sal - va - tion. Al - le - lu - ia.

- lu - ia. Al - le - lu - ia.

40. SILENT NIGHT

Words by JOSEF MOHR,
tr. DAVID WILLCOCKS

FRANZ GRUBER
arranged by DAVID WILLCOCKS

This setting may more effectively be sung a semitone lower.

v. 1: straight on
v. 3: on to p. 187

SOPRANO

mp

1. Sleep in hea - ven-ly peace.
3. Christ th'in - car - nate God.

A.

Ah *Ah*

T.

pp

ho - ly child.
- demp - tion and grace,

Ah

B.

p

Ah *Ah* *Ah*

S.

1st time

A.

pp *pochiss.* *sim.*

Ah *Ah* Al - le - lu - ia al - le - lu - ia

T.

p

Sleep__ in hea - ven-ly peace.

B.

pp *pochiss.* *sim.*

__ *Ah*__ *Ah* Al - le - lu - ia al - le - lu - ia

dal ℅ for v. 3

Christ our Sa-viour is here,___ Christ our Sa-viour is here.___

Christ our Sa-viour is here,___ Christ our Sa-viour is here.___

Christ our Sa-viour is here,___ Christ our Sa-viour is here.___

Christ our Sa-viour is here,___ Christ our Sa-viour is here.___

Christ our Sa-viour is here, Christ our Sa-viour is here.___

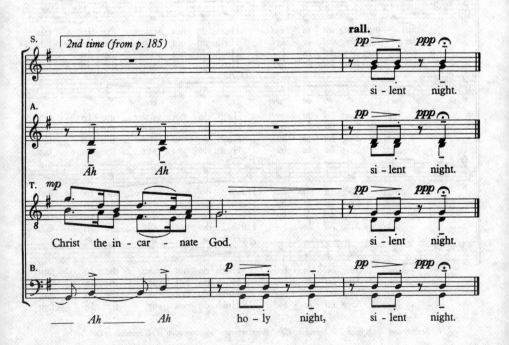

S. *2nd time (from p. 185)*

si - lent night.

A.

Ah Ah si - lent night.

T. Christ the in-car - nate God. si - lent night.

B. ___ Ah ___ Ah ho-ly night, si - lent night.

41. THE INFANT KING

Words by
S. BARING-GOULD

Basque Noël
arranged by DAVID WILLCOCKS

Melody and words from *The University Carol Book*, reprinted by permission of H. Freeman & Co.

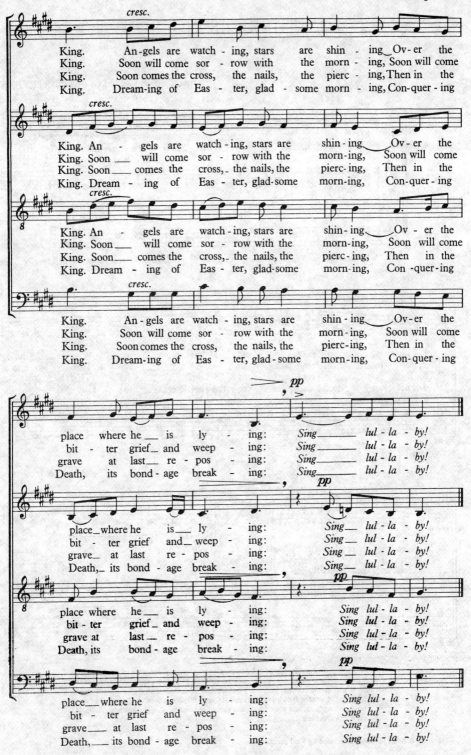

42. THERE IS NO ROSE

Anonymous, c. 1420
transcribed and edited by JOHN STEVENS

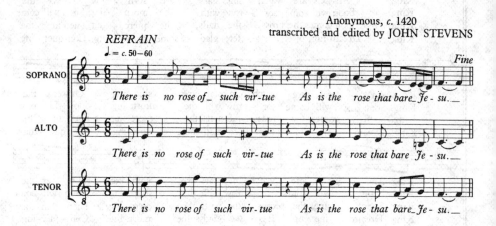

Note by John Stevens:
From a MS. roll of carols, copied out in the early 15th century and now in the Library of Trinity College, Cambridge; printed by kind permission. The carol begins and ends with the refrain (the alto part is editorial and may be omitted at will); the verses are for soloists. Small accidentals in the refrain are absent from the MS. and may be ignored if desired. The tenor has the tune throughout, and the other voices should be subordinate. The music was intended to be sung unaccompanied.

43. GABRIEL'S MESSAGE

Words by
S. BARING-GOULD

Basque carol
arranged by DAVID WILLCOCKS

Melody and words from *The University Carol Book*, reprinted by permission of H. Freeman & Co.

soul shall laud and mag - ni - fy His Ho - ly Name.' — Most
Chris - tian folk through-out the world will ev - er say:___

God, My soul shall mag - ni - fy His Ho - ly
morn, And folk through - out the world will ev - er

God, My soul shall laud___ and mag - ni - fy His
morn, And folk, and folk___ through-out the world will

God, My soul shall mag - ni - fy His
morn, And folk through - out___ the world will

Repeat for v. 4

high - ly fa - vour'd la - dy, *Glo - - - ri - a!*

Name.' — Most high - ly fa - vour'd la - dy, *Glo - ri - a!*
say:___

Ho - ly Name.' ___ *Glo - - ri - a!*
ev - er say:___

Ho - ly Name.' *Glo - - - ri - a!*
ev - er say:

44. THE HOLLY AND THE IVY

English traditional carol
arranged by H. WALFORD DAVIES

First four verses

deer,   The play-ing of the mer - ry or - gan,   Sweet sing-ing in__ the__ choir.

deer,   The play - ing of__ the   mer-ry or-gan,   Sweet sing-ing in   the   choir.

deer,   The play - ing of   the or - gan,   Sweet sing-ing in__ the__ choir.

deer,__ The play-ing of   the   or - gan,   Sweet sing-ing in__ the   choir.

First four verses

Last verse

sing - ing,__ sweet__ sing - - - ing in_____ the__ choir.

sing - ing, sweet   sing - - - ing in_____ the   choir.

sing - ing,__ sweet__ sing - - - ing in_____ the__ choir.

sing - ing,__ sweet   sing - - - ing in_____ the   choir.

Last verse

45. THE LORD AT FIRST DID ADAM MAKE

English traditional carol
arranged by DAVID WILLCOCKS

1. The Lord at first did A - dam make Out of the dust and clay,
And in his nos - trils breath - ed life E'en as the scrip - tures say.
And then in E - den's pa - ra - dise He pla - ced him to dwell, That
he with - in it should re - main, To dress and keep it well:
Now let good Chris - tians all be - gin An ho - ly life to live, And
to re - joice and mer - ry be, For this is Christ - mas Eve.

2. And thus with - in the gar - den he Was set there - in to stay;
And in com - mand - ment un - to him These words the Lord did say:

ORGAN
Ch. Flutes

Also available separately (X198)

TENORS and BASSES

mf

'The fruit which in the gar-den grows To thee shall be for meat, Ex-

Sw. diap.

(Ped. optional)

-cept the tree in the midst there-of, Of which thou shalt not eat:'

TENORS

mf

Ah____ Ah____

BARITONES

f

Now let good Chris-tians all be-gin An ho-ly life to live, And

BASSES *mf*

(Organ tacet) Ah____ Ah____

to re-joice and__ mer-ry be, For this is Christ-mas Eve.

TENORS and BASSES

3. 'For_ in the day thou shalt it touch Or dost to it come nigh,
If_ so thou do but_ eat there-of Then thou shalt sure - ly die.'

SOPRANOS

But A - dam he did_ take no heed Un - to that on - ly thing, But

did trans - gress God's ho - ly law, And so was wrapt in sin:

SOPRANOS

Now let good Chris - tians all be - gin An ho - ly life to live, And

ALTOS

(Organ tacet) Ah _____ Ah____

to re - joice and_ mer - ry be, For this is Christ - mas Eve.

ALL VOICES

CHOIR I

CHOIR II
and
ORGAN

S.

A.

T.

B.

4. Now mark the good-ness of the Lord, Which he for man-kind bore;
His mer-cy soon he did ex-tend, Lost man for to re-store;

Ah

mf And then, for to re-deem our souls From death and hell-ish thrall, He
f Now let good Chris-tians all be-gin An ho-ly life to live, And

1st time: *mf*
2nd time: *f*

Ah

Ah

Ah

1st time: *mf* (Organ tacet)
2nd time: *f*

2nd time: rall. e cresc.

said his own dear Son should be The Sa-viour of us all:
to re-joice and mer-ry be, For this is Christ-mas Eve.

2nd time: rall. e cresc.

Ah

Ah

Ah

Ah

Ah

46. THE TRUTH FROM ABOVE

English traditional carol
arranged by R. VAUGHAN WILLIAMS

1. This is the truth sent from a - bove, The
2. The first thing which I do re - late

truth of God, the God of love, There-fore don't turn me
Is that God did man cre - ate; The next thing which to

from your door, But heark-en all both rich and poor.
you I'll tell Wo - man was made with man to dwell.

3. Thus we were heirs to endless woes,
Till God the Lord did interpose;
And so a promise soon did run
That he would redeem us by his Son.

4. And at that season of the year
Our blest Redeemer did appear;
He here did live, and here did preach,
And many thousands he did teach.

5. Thus he in love to us behaved,
To show us how we must be saved;
And if you want to know the way,
Be pleased to hear what he did say.

47. TOMORROW SHALL BE MY DANCING DAY

English traditional carol
arranged by DAVID WILLCOCKS

Also available separately (X141)

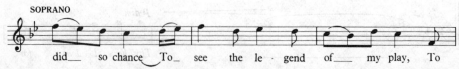

48. WHILE SHEPHERDS WATCHED THEIR FLOCKS

Words by
NAHUM TATE (1652–1715)

Este's Psalter, 1592
Descant and organ part by DAVID WILLCOCKS

3. 'To you in David's town this day
   Is born of David's line
   A Saviour, who is Christ the Lord;
   And this shall be the sign:

4. 'The heavenly Babe you there shall find
   To human view displayed,
   All meanly wrapped in swathing bands,
   And in a manger laid.'

5. Thus spake the Seraph; and forthwith
   Appeared a shining throng
   Of angels praising God, who thus
   Addressed their joyful song:

Also available separately (*Six Christmas Hymns* arr. David Willcocks)

49. PATAPAN

Words by
LA MONNOYE
tr. PERCY DEARMER

Burgundian tune
arranged by REGINALD JACQUES

1. Wil - lie, take your lit - tle drum, With your whis - tle, Rob - in, come! When we hear the fife and drum,
2. Thus the men of old - en days Loved the King of kings to praise: When they hear the fife and drum,
3. God and man are now be - come More at one than fife and drum. When you hear the fife and drum,

Tu - re - lu - re

Melody and words from *The Oxford Book of Carols*
Also available separately (T86)

- lu,   pat - a -pat - a - pan,

When we   hear the fife and
When they hear the fife and
When you   hear the fife and

Tu - re - lu - re - lu,

drum, Christ - mas should be___ fro - lic - some.
drum, Sure our child - ren___ won't___ be___ dumb!
drum, Dance, and make the___ vil - lage___ hum!

Small notes last time

★Piano plays small notes when no flute etc. available

50. ZION HEARS THE WATCHMEN'S VOICES

P. NICOLAI (1556–1608)
English words by JOHN RUTTER

J. S. BACH
(from Cantata 140)
edited by JOHN RUTTER

(Andante con moto)

PIANO or ORGAN
(orig. strings and continuo)

Small notes, crossed slurs, and bracketed dynamics and ornaments are editorial. A few discrepancies of figuring and ornamentation in the repeated section have been eliminated. Where the accompaniment is played on the organ, the melody should be picked out on a separate manual and small notes transposed up an octave where appropriate (a fully-realised continuo part is available with the orchestral hire material). Bass part has been transposed down an octave in the two sections marked ⌊___⌋. The closing chorale may effectively follow straight on from this movement.

Also available separately (X212)

Lyrics (measure 20(41), 1st time):
She ea - ger wakes to____ greet the day.
sie wa - chet und steht____ ei - lend auf.
Her day - star
ihr Licht wird

Lyrics (measure 23, 2nd time):
dawns with __ bright-est ray.
hell, ihr____ Stern geht auf.

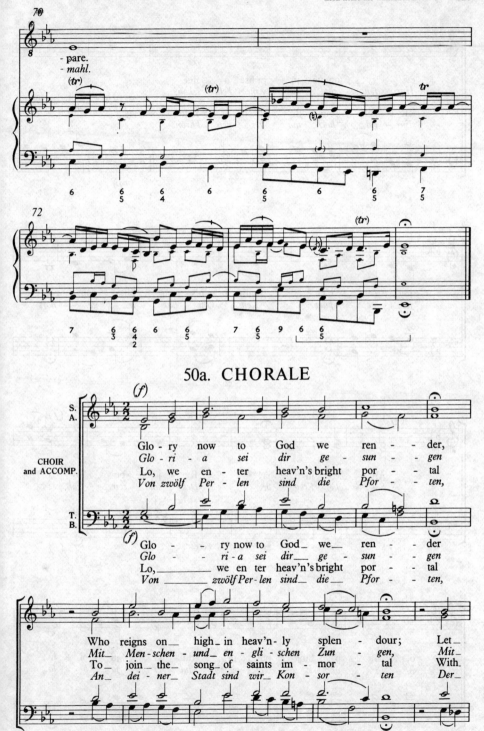

50a. CHORALE

Glo - ry now to God we ren - - der,
Glo - ri - a sei dir ge - sun - - gen
Lo, we en - ter heav'n's bright por - - tal
Von zwölf Per - len sind die Pfor - - ten,

Glo - - ry now to God_ we_ ren - - der
Glo - - ri - a sei dir_ ge - sun - - gen
Lo,_____ we en ter heav'n's bright por - - tal
Von _____ zwölf Per - len sind die_ Pfor - - ten,

Who reigns on_ high in heav'n - ly splen - dour; Let_
*Mit_ Men - schen - und_ en - gli - schen Zun - gen, Mit_*
To_ join the_ song of saints im - mor - tal With_
*An dei - ner_ Stadt sind wir Kon - sor - ten Der_*

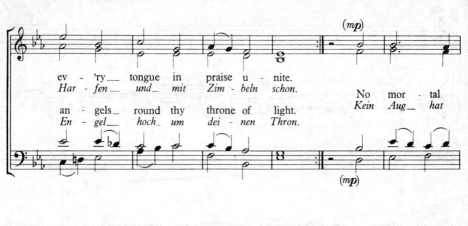

ev - 'ry___ tongue in praise u - nite.
Har - fen___ und___ mit Zim - beln schon.

an - gels___ round thy throne of light.
En - gel___ hoch um dei - nen Thron.

No mor - tal hat
Kein Aug___ hat

joy___ can___ e'er with___ heav'n's true bliss___ com - pare;
je___ ge - spürt, Kein___ Ohr hat je___ ge - hört

Al - le - lu - ia! Re - joice_ be - low, i -
Sol - che Freu - de. Des sind___ wir___ froh, i -

-o, i - o! Sing___ out in___ dul - ci ju - bi - lo.
-o, i - o! E - wig___ in___ dul - ci ju - bi - lo.

App. 1. HARK! THE HERALD ANGELS SING

Words by C. WESLEY,
T. WHITEFIELD, M. MADAN
and others

MENDELSSOHN,
adapted by W. H. CUMMINGS

1. Hark! the herald angels sing — Glory to the new-born King;
2. Christ, by highest heav'n adored, — Christ, the ever-lasting Lord,
3. Hail the heav'n-born Prince of Peace! — Hail the Sun of Righteous-ness!

Peace on earth and mercy mild, — God and sinners reconciled:
Late in time behold him come — Off-spring of a virgin's womb:
Light and life to all he brings, — Ris'n with healing in his wings;

Joyful all ye nations rise, — Join the triumph of the skies, —
Veiled in flesh the Godhead see, — Hail th'in-car-nate De-i-ty! —
Mild he lays his glory by, — Born that man no more may die, —

With th'an-ge-lic host proclaim, — Christ is — born in Bethlehem.
Pleased as man with man to dwell, — Je-sus, — our Em-ma-nu-el.
Born to raise the sons of earth, — Born to — give them se-cond birth.

UNISON

Hark! the herald angels sing — Glory — to the new-born King.

Org.

Org. ped.

Deity pronounced Dee-ity

App. 2. O COME, ALL YE FAITHFUL
(Adeste fideles)

Words by J. F. WADE
tr. F. OAKELEY, W. T. BROOKE
and others

Melody by
J. F. WADE (c. 1711–1786)

1. O come, all ye faithful, Joyful and triumphant, O come ye, O come ye to Bethlehem; Come and behold him Born the King of Angels: O come, let us adore him, O come, let us adore him, O come, let us adore him, Christ the Lord!

2. God of God, Light of Light, Lo! he abhors not the Virgin's womb; Very God, Begotten, not created:

3. See how the shepherds, Summoned to his cradle, Leaving their flocks, draw nigh with lowly fear; We too will thither Bend our joyful footsteps:

4. Sing, choirs of angels, Sing in exultation, Sing, all ye citizens of heav'n above; Glory to God In the highest:

Harmony from *The English Hymnal*
For extended version arranged by David Willcocks, see *Carols for Choirs 1.*

AN ADVENT CAROL SERVICE

¶ *The Congregation shall stand while the Choir sings the* Matin Responsory *at the West End of the Church, followed by the hymn* Come, thou Redeemer of the earth *in procession to the Choir stalls.*

¶ *All shall then be bidden to prayer in these words:*

BELOVED in Christ, as we await the great festival of Christmas let us prepare ourselves so that we may be shown its true meaning. Let us hear, in lessons from Holy Scripture, how the prophets of Israel foretold that God would visit and redeem his waiting people. Let us rejoice, in our carols and hymns, that the good purpose of God is being mightily fulfilled. Let us celebrate the promise that our Lord and Saviour, Jesus Christ, will bring all men and all things into the glory of God's eternal kingdom. The blind receive their sight, and the lame walk, the lepers are cleansed, and the deaf hear, the dead are raised up, and the poor have the Gospel preached to them.

But first, let us pray for the world which God so loves, for those who have not heard the good news of God, or who do not believe it; for those who walk in darkness and the shadow of death; and for the Church in this place and everywhere, that it may be freed from all evil and fear, and may in pure joy lift up the light of the love of God.

These prayers and praises let us humbly offer to God, in the words which Christ himself taught us:

Our Father, which [who] art in heaven, hallowed be thy name; thy kingdom come; thy will be done; in [on] earth as it is in heaven. Give us this day our daily bread. And forgive us our trespasses, as we forgive them that [those who] trespass against us. And lead us not into temptation; But deliver us from evil. For thine is the kingdom, the power, and the glory, for ever and ever. Amen.

¶ *Then shall the Congregation sit.*
[*The Readers of the Lessons should be appointed after a definite order; in a Cathedral, for instance, from a Chorister up to a Bishop.*
Each Reader should proceed to the Reading Desk at the beginning of the last verse of the preceding carol or hymn; and announce his Lesson by the descriptive sentence attached to it. At the end of the Lesson, the Reader should pause and say: Thanks be to God.]

FIRST LESSON
The Prophet proclaims good news to a people in exile.   ISAIAH XL, 1–8

SECOND LESSON
The Lord promises to send his people a righteous King.   JEREMIAH XXIII, 5–6

THIRD LESSON
The Lord promises that the King will come to Israel in peace.   ZECHARIAH IX, 9–10

FOURTH LESSON
The Prophet foretells the advent of the desire of all nations.   HAGGAI II, 6–9

FIFTH LESSON
The Prophet foretells the glory of the kingdom of God.   ISAIAH XXXV, 1–6

SIXTH LESSON
The angel Gabriel salutes the Blessed Virgin Mary. ST LUKE I, 26–35, 38

ALTERNATIVE SIXTH LESSON
St Paul declares the good purpose of God. ROMANS VIII, 28–39

℣ *The Congregation shall stand for the seventh lesson.*
SEVENTH LESSON
Jesus proclaims the coming of the kingdom of God. ST MARK I, 1–15

VESPER RESPONSORY
℣ *To be said by Priest and People, alternately*

Priest   Judah and Jerusalem, fear not, nor be dismayed;
People   Tomorrow go ye forth, and the Lord, he will be with you.
Priest   Stand ye still, and ye shall see the salvation of the Lord.
People   Tomorrow go ye forth, and the Lord, he will be with you.
Priest   Glory be to the Father, and to the Son, and to the Holy Ghost.
People   Tomorrow go ye forth, and the Lord, he will be with you.

℣ *All shall keep silence for a time.*

COLLECT
Priest   We wait for thy loving kindness, O Lord.
People   In the midst of thy temple.

Let us pray.

O God, who makest us glad with the yearly expectation of thy coming, Grant that we, who with joy receive thy only-begotten Son as our Redeemer, may without fear behold him when he shall come to be our Judge, even thy Son our Lord Jesus Christ; who liveth and reigneth with thee and the Holy Ghost, one God, world without end. *Amen.*

THE BLESSING
Go forth into the world in peace; be of good courage; hold fast that which is good; render to no man evil for evil; strengthen the faint-hearted; support the weak; help the afflicted; honour all men; love and serve the Lord, rejoicing in the power of the Holy Spirit.

And the blessing of God Almighty, the Father, the Son, and the Holy Spirit, be upon you, and remain with you for ever. *Amen.*